You Can Write

COOL

Poems

by Jennifer Fandel

Consultant:
Terry Flaherty, PhD
Professor of English
Minnesota State University, Mankato

CAPSTONE PRESS
a capstone imprint

First Facts is published by Capstone Press,
1710 Roe Crest Drive, North Mankato, Minnesota 56003
www.capstonepub.com

Library of Congress Cataloging-in-Publication Data
Fandel, Jennifer.
  You can write cool poems / by Jennifer Fandel.
    p. cm.
  Includes index.
  Summary: "Introduces readers to the key steps in writing a poem through the use of
examples and exercises"—Provided by publisher.
  ISBN 978-1-4296-7616-8 (library binding)
  ISBN 978-1-4296-7961-9 (paperback)
  1. Poetry—Authorship—Juvenile literature. I. Title.
PN1042.F36 2012
808.1—dc23   2011035761

Editorial Credits
Jill Kalz, editor; Juliette Peters, designer; Kathy McColley, production specialist

Photo Credits
Shutterstock: 3445128471, 12, Anat-oli, 10 (pig), Blend Images, 16 (boy), Brad Wynnyk, 14,
Chas, cover (marker), Craig Wactor, 3, 18 (bee), 23, Eric Isselée, 7, Gaby Kooijman, 17, Golden
Pixels LLC, 16 (swimmers), GSPhotography, 5, Hue Chee Kong, 8, jeka84, 13 (clouds), Kesu,
cover (bettle), Ljupco Smokovski, 18 (honey), naluwan, 20, Nils Z, 11, Nixx Photography, 6,
Noam Armonn, 9, Papik, 16 (snail), RazvanZinica, 19, ref348985, 18 (honeycomb), Smit, 10
(bike), Thomas M Perkins, 21, Triff, cover (clouds), Ultrashock, 15, 24 (porcupine), WilleeCole,
15 (duck), Willem Havenaar, 13 (ball)

Artistic Effects
Shutterstock: Triff

TABLE of CONTENTS

The Art of Poetry

Some people make art with clay. Others use metal, stone, or paper. Musicians make art with sounds. Poets use words.

Poems are like songs without music. The words can talk about any subject. They can tell stories or talk about feelings, such as love or sadness. Poems can be long or short. Some rhyme. Others don't. There are no right or wrong poems.

rhyme—to have word endings that sound the same

Loud and Clear DETAILS

All poets want to be understood. Details help. Details give readers the full picture.

To you, a dog may be a small, fluffy white toy. To others, it may be a big, smooth-haired hunter with floppy ears. Be clear when you write.

Use details.

detail—a fact about an object

Pick a subject, such as a cat. In two minutes, list as many details as you can about it. Use the following questions as guides.

How does it look?

Smell?

Sound?

Feel?

Taste?

What does it do?

How does it act?

Ask a friend to do the same exercise. Then compare both lists. How are they different?

FAST FACT

You understand the world through your five senses—sight, smell, taste, touch, and hearing. How many senses are you using right now?

FREE VERSE

All poems have a shape. **Free verse** is a form of poetry with no rules. Lines can be long or short. You can move them wherever you like. Words may rhyme or not. It's up to you!

Hello and Good-bye
The orange bug
with six hairy legs
chirped like a bird
then flew far away.

Hello and Good-bye
The orange bug with six hairy legs
chirped like a bird then flew far away.

Hello and Good-bye
the orange bug
with six hairy legs
chirped
like a bird then
flew far away

8

free verse—a form of poetry without rules

Write a free-verse poem about a food, such as spaghetti. Use details. Is the sauce thin and red or thick and white? Do the spaghetti noodles feel slippery or sticky? Can you see chunky pieces of tomato or greasy meatballs?

Spaghetti
I eat worms
long skinny worms
slippery worms
with spicy red sauce
I slurp them up
YUM!

9

Is It My Imagination? IMAGERY

The **brakes** on your bike squeal like **piglets**.
The cheese smells like gym socks.
The drum rumbles as loudly as thunder.

Poetry is made of **imagery**. Imagery is a word picture. Words on the page create pictures in readers' minds. But the pictures aren't just things to see. Readers may hear, smell, taste, and feel imagery too.

imagery—details that make a picture in your mind

Pick a subject, such as a glass of juice.
Then fill in these blanks:

The _____ (subject) smells like _____.
It looks like _____.
It tastes like _____.
It feels like _____.
It sounds like _____.

FAST FACT

Similes (SIM-uh-leez) and metaphors (MET-uh-forz) are types of imagery. Similes use the words "like" or "as" to connect different things ("growls like a dog" or "goofy as a monkey"). Metaphors connect ideas by saying something IS something ("his head is a melon").

Full of Surprises

You walk into a dark room and **BOO!** Your little sister scares you.

Surprises are hard to forget. When writing, surprise readers with fresh, new details. They will want to read more. And your words will stick in their minds.

People often say that the sun looks like a yellow ball. But what else does it remind you of? How does the heat feel on your skin? Everyone sees the world differently. List five details to describe the sun. Which ones surprise you the most?

the sun is a bright jewel

the sun is a gold coin

the sun is a yellow blister

the sun feels like a wool blanket

the sun looks like an egg yolk

Poetry Action — STRONG VERBS

Rain **sizzles** on the hot street.
Prairie dogs **pop** out of the ground.
The river *roars*.

"Sizzle," "pop," and "roar" are active **verbs**. They describe actions. Active verbs make poems come to life.

The car doesn't ***move*** down the street. It *zips*.
The girl doesn't ***eat*** her lunch. She **gobbles** it.

verb—a word that expresses action

Pick an animal, such as a porcupine or a duck. Then pick active verbs to describe how it moves. Use these verbs in a free-verse poem.

saunters   **slides**   **sneaks**

First Steps
My baby sister <u>wiggles</u>
and <u>waggles</u> when she walks.
She <u>waddles</u> like a duck.
Quack! Quack! Quack!

15

Fun with Sound

The boy bounces the basketball.

Snails slide in their shiny shells.

In the summer, it's cool in the pool.

Sounds make readers feel a poem. Hear how the s sound slides across the page. Feel the bounce of the b sounds. Listen to the way the oo sounds chill out!

16

List words that have the letter P in them—at the start, middle, or end. Then write a free-verse poem using as many of those P words as you can. Listen to how the letter P pops on the page.

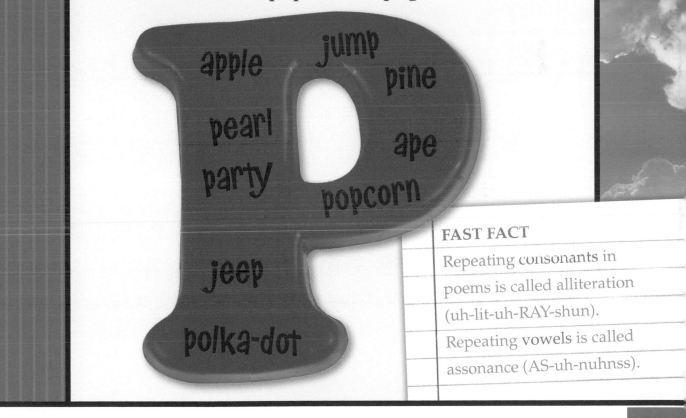

apple
jump
pine
pearl
ape
party
popcorn
jeep
polka-dot

FAST FACT

Repeating consonants in poems is called alliteration (uh-lit-uh-RAY-shun). Repeating **vowels** is called assonance (AS-uh-nuhnss).

consonant—a letter that isn't a vowel

vowel—the letters A, E, I, O, U, and sometimes Y

Shape Up — FORMAL POETRY

Unlike free verse, formal poetry has rules. The rules often help poets make new discoveries.

Some formal poems rhyme at the end of each line. The sounds echo.

You're welcome, said the bee.
The honey came from me.

Other poems follow a clear **rhythm**. The stresses in words give each line a beat.

LON-don BRIDGE is FALL-ing DOWN.

Still others count the number of **syllables** on each line.

---

rhythm—a beat

syllable—a unit of sound in a word

Exercise

Haiku are formal three-line poems. They look closely at one subject. The first line has five syllables. The second line has seven syllables. The last line has five syllables. Follow the example, and write a haiku about your favorite animal.

1   2 3   4   5
The lizard zooms by.

1 2   3   4   5 6 7
Desert sand burns his belly.

1   2   3   4   5
All he wants is shade.

Time to Fine-Tune REVISING

Sometimes your poems are great right away. But most of the time, you'll need to **revise**. You want everyone to understand your poem.

Trade your poems with a friend. Read each other's poems. Share what you liked best. Then share what you didn't understand. Don't be afraid to revise. Revising usually makes poems better.

revise—to change to make better

Playing with words can be a lot of fun. How many poems will you write today?

The clouds above me make me happy

Glossary

consonant (KON-suh-nuhnt)—a letter of the alphabet that isn't a vowel

detail (DEE-tayl)—one of many facts about an item

formal (FOR-muhl)—following fixed rules and forms

free verse (FREE VURSS)—a poetic form that has no rules about subject, length, or style

imagery (IM-ij-ree)—details that make a picture in readers' minds

revise (ri-VIZE)—to change to make better or clearer

rhyme (RIME)—to have word endings that sound the same, such as "light" and "fight"

rhythm (RITH-uhm)—a regular pattern of beats

syllable (SIL-uh-buhl)—a unit of sound in a word; "syllable" is made of three syl-la-bles

verb (VURB)—a word used to express an action or condition

vowel (VOU-uhl)—the letters A, E, I, O, U, and sometimes Y

Read More

Loewen, Nancy. *Words, Wit, and Wonder: Writing Your Own Poem.* Writer's Toolbox. Minneapolis: Picture Window Books, 2009.

Minden, Cecilia, and Kate Roth. *How to Write a Poem.* Language Arts Explorer Junior. Ann Arbor, Mich.: Cherry Lake Pub., 2011.

Salas, Laura Purdie. *A Fuzzy-Fast Blur: Poems about Pets.* Poetry. Mankato, Minn.: Capstone Press, 2009.

Internet Sites

FactHound offers a safe, fun way to find Internet sites related to this book. All of the sites on FactHound have been researched by our staff.

Here's all you do:

Visit *www.facthound.com*

Type in this code: 9781429676168

Super-cool stuff!

Check out projects, games and lots more at
www.capstonekids.com

Index